GW00702172

EAST ANGLIA

CONTENTS

MYRIAD
LONDON

Constable Country

Flatford Mill and the village of Dedham lie in glorious Dedham Vale, known as Constable Country in memory of the famous landscape painter, a native of the area.

Flatford Mill lies at the heart of Constable Country, in the Dedham Vale, on the river Stour in Suffolk. Constable's family owned the mill at Flatford and, as a boy, the painter spent a great deal of time there learning the family trade. Many of the buildings around the mill featured in Constable's idyllic pastoral paintings. Probably his most famous, *The Hay Wain*, depicts Willy Lott's cottage (above). Willy Lott was one of the mill-hands who worked at Flatford. The mill buildings are now owned by the National Trust and Bridge Cottage (far left) has an exhibition of the painter's life.

DEDHAM This pretty village is located on the Essex bank of the river Stour opposite Flatford and it has many associations with Constable. In the Middle Ages Dedham prospered as a wool town and many of the fine buildings in the village date from this era, including the half-timbered Marlborough Head Hotel (above) in the town centre. Dedham Hall (left), a splendid Georgian building and now a private house, was the old grammar school where Constable studied; he walked here each day from his home at East Bergholt. Dedham is an ideal starting point for a stroll along the banks of the river to Flatford Mill, the scene of many of Constable's best-known paintings. The church of St Mary the Virgin (right) was a favourite of Constable and often features in his work. It has one of Constable's few religious paintings, *The Ascension*, which hangs in the nave opposite the north porch.

The shields mounted on the nave roof below show *The Mayflower* and commemorate links with Dedham, Massachusetts where many local people emigrated. Also shown are the arms of Elizabeth 1 – Dedham was at the centre of Sabbatarian debates during her tumultuous reign.

Colchester

A military garrison since Roman times
and Britain's most ancient town.

The capital of Roman Britain, Colchester is Britain's oldest recorded town. Its castle (left) was built on the site of the Roman temple of Claudius by William the Conqueror. It houses an award-winning museum with many hands-on displays which illustrate Colchester's history from the Stone Age to the Civil War. Tymperleys Clock Museum (below) is housed in a 15th-century timber-framed building, once the home of William Gilberd, physician to Queen Elizabeth I. The clocks on display were made in Colchester between 1640-1860. Colchester Town Hall's 162ft Victoria Tower (right) dominates the high street. The statue at the top is of St Helena, patron saint of Colchester.

Essex Coast

The Essex coastline is dotted with rivers and creeks graced with beautiful towns and villages such as Maldon.

Brightlingsea (above) is situated between the towns of Colchester and Clacton at the mouth of the river Colne. The town is the only Cinque Port in Essex. In the centre of the town is the 600 year old Jacob's Hall, one of the oldest timber-framed buildings in England. The waterfront boasts colourful beach huts, a lively sailing scene and an attractive small beach which looks across to Mersea Island. At the Aldous Heritage Dock many historic fishing smacks can be seen; the town has a thriving preservation society which cares for these attractive boats and organises regular races on the Colne – a tradition which dates back to the late 18th century.

MALDON This historic hill town (right) stands at the head of the Blackwater Estuary and is home to many historic Thames sailing barges which can be seen regularly moored up by the Jolly Sailor Inn at the quay (left) in Maldon. These boats were once the maritime workhorses of eastern England and were used to carry cargo, including hay, from the farmlands of Essex to London as feed and bedding for horses – they were often called "haystackers" due to the piles of hay on deck. The boats were built with flat bottoms so that they could rest up in the muddy creeks and inlets of the Essex coast at low tide. These days the graceful barges with their traditional tan sails earn their living carrying passengers on leisure trips. The estuary has a well-earned reputation for wildlife. Vast numbers of birds are attracted to the area each year, where they take shelter through the winter.

TOLLESBURY Tollesbury is often referred to as the village of the "Plough and Sail", because it relied on the harvest of both the land and the sea. It is an attractive village situated on the north bank of the Blackwater Estuary, between Maldon and West Mersea and overlooks coastal marshlands. The settlement expanded rapidly in the late 19th and 20th centuries, and the countryside around the village (which is a conservation area) has changed constantly over the last two centuries, as the marshlands have been drained and embankments constructed. The restored wooden sail lofts (below) were used to store equipment for Edwardian racing yachts. At the centre of the village is The Square. On the west side stands the King's Head, the seafarers' pub; opposite is the church of St Mary the Virgin, dating from around 1090.

MISTLEY North-east of Colchester, on the southern bank of the Stour estuary this village (above) grew rapidly in the 18th century, thanks to local landowner Richard Rigby who wanted to establish a spa town. He employed a number of prominent architects including Robert Adam but the plans collapsed when Rigby mismanaged his position as Paymaster of the Forces. Two of Adam's designs can still be seen: Mistley Towers, the unusual twin constructions designed to sit at either end of the new church of St Mary the Virgin (never built due to Rigby's financial collapse) and the Swan Basin in the High Street opposite the Thorn Hotel. Close to Dedham Vale, the town is a gateway to Constable Country.

CLACTON The one time sleepy fishing village of Clacton (left and above) blossomed in the late 1900s when Peter Schuyler Bruff, an engineer and manager of the Eastern Union Railway, built a pier which gave access to London by boat. He supervised the wooden pier's construction and it opened in 1871. It soon became a popular attraction for promenading, not just a place for landing goods and passengers. Pier improvements continued during the 20th century and the Ocean Theatre opened in 1928. Today Clacton is a lively resort at the heart of the "Essex Sunshine Coast".

FRINTON This north Essex coastal town shares a clean sandy beach with Clacton and Walton. This extends from Colne Point in the south to Walton-on-the-Naze – the "Naze" is a natural headland which protrudes into the North Sea. Frinton developed as a planned seaside resort between 1890-1900 and it rapidly became a fashionable place to visit during the Edwardian era, when the golf and tennis clubs were frequented by the international high society set; Connaught Avenue, the main entry to the seafront, became known as "the Bond Street of East Anglia". The unusual beach huts (above) stretch from Frinton northwards to the far side of Walton.

The handsome town of Thaxted, north-east of Stansted, contains a famous Guildhall and winding streets lined with medieval houses which seem to lead towards the cathedral-like church of St John. Originally a town of thatchers, which gave the town its name, Thaxted subsequently became a centre of the cloth and cutlery trades. The town is the spiritual home of Morris dancing. The revival of this traditional pursuit was begun locally in 1911 by Mrs Miriam Noel, wife of the local vicar, Fr Conrad Noel. Today the Morris Men dance traditional Cotswold dances in Thaxted and its surrounding villages and towns between May and September. The annual gathering of Morris Men from all over England (below) is an amazing spectacle.

LOWE'S MILL The striking tower mill (above) was built in 1804 by John Webb, to help feed the growing population of London. The bricks came from Webb's brick and tileworks. The walls are 4ft thick at the base and 18 inches thick at bin floor level. Towards the end of the 19th century it had become uneconomic and in 1904 it was closed down and its sails locked up. The mill now houses an agricultural museum.

THE CHANTRY These two attractive buildings (right) are located in the churchyard of St John the Baptist. The thatched building originally served as accommodation for the priest and dates back to the 16th century. The building to its right stands on the site of a former chantry house. Now immaculately restored, for more than 150 years or both buildings have served as almshouses for elderly people.

Rural Essex

The north of the county is famed for its exquisite villages and pretty countryside.

FINCHINGFIELD This picture postcard village (right and below) is situated between Sible Hedingham and Thaxted on the Braintree to Saffron Walden road. The name dates back to Saxon times when Finc's folk made a clearing in the forest for a new settlement. William the Conqueror gave the village to Roger Bigod for his services during the invasion. It has a green, duckpond and a windmill, together with several medieval houses known as *cabbaches*. Many of the cottages have pargetting on their walls which is very characteristic of the area. The unusual tower of the beautiful church of St John (below) with its cupola looms over the village and the streets around the church provide an ideal vantage point to look down on the picturesque village green and the narrow bridge which straddles the stream. The Causeway Tea Cottage (below) is a popular stop for visitors. The cottage was built in 1490, two years before Columbus discovered America. It is easy to see why Finchingfield is often described as the most photographed village in all of Essex.

CASTLE HEDINGHAM This historic village is situated just west of Halstead and is best known for its magnificent Norman keep. Built in 1140 by Aubrey de Vere, earl of Oxford, this is one of the best preserved castle keeps in Europe. Aubrey de Vere, one of William the Conqueror's main supporters, built Castle Hedingham on land granted to him by William for his support during the invasion of England. The keep is the only medieval part of the castle to survive and today it forms a superb background for jousting tournaments where history is brought to life with spectacular re-enactments featuring knights in armed combat, music, entertainment and dancing. The castle is surrounded by a beautiful old deer park with a 15th century Tudor bridge which replaced the castle drawbridge and spans the now dry moat leading to the inner bailey. The park has an unusual dovecote and attractive lake. Castle Hedingham is home to the Colne Valley and Halstead Railway which was founded in 1974. It runs steam trains on a mile-long track along the Colne valley, once part of the original railway started in 1856 between Halstead and Haverhill. The twin village of Sible Hedingham lies to the south on the opposite bank of the river Colne.

ASHDON The village of Ashdon, located three miles north-east of Saffron Waldon, lies on an ancient road within the picturesque rolling hills of the boulder clays of north-east Essex. It is surrounded by lush arable land and large areas of what was once a vast forest. All Saints Church (left) was rebuilt in stone in the early 11th century. Ashdon is host to a kite festival which is held at Waltons Park each year in early June. The Ashdon Village Collection, in Church Hill, is a museum of village life through the ages. Its fascinating displays cover agriculture, the home, fashion, shopping and entertainment.

AUDLEY END This superb Jacobean house stands on the site of the former Benedictine monastery of Walden Abbey. It is an early 17th-century country mansion, and was first granted to Sir Thomas Audley in 1538 by Henry VIII. Thomas Audley's grandson Thomas, first Earl of Suffolk, rebuilt the mansion between 1610 and 1614. The house is now only about one third of its original size. During the middle ages, the gardens and grounds around Audley End House were the cultivated estate of an abbey. In the 18th century the magnificent park was transformed from its formal design into one of "Capability" Brown's most stunning and successful pastoral landscapes. The parkland and Victorian gardens around the house have recently been restored and an artificial lake constructed, fed by the river Cam.

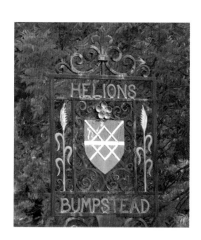

ESSEX VILLAGE SIGNS There are few areas of Britain that have such a strong tradition of painted village signs than Essex and this is particularly true of the more rural areas in the north of the county. The signs usully depict key events in the history of the village and notable local landmarks. Seen here are the signs for Ridgewell (left) in north-west Essex near the Suffolk border, Helions Bumpstead (below left) and White Colne (below) in the Colne valley north-west of Colchester.

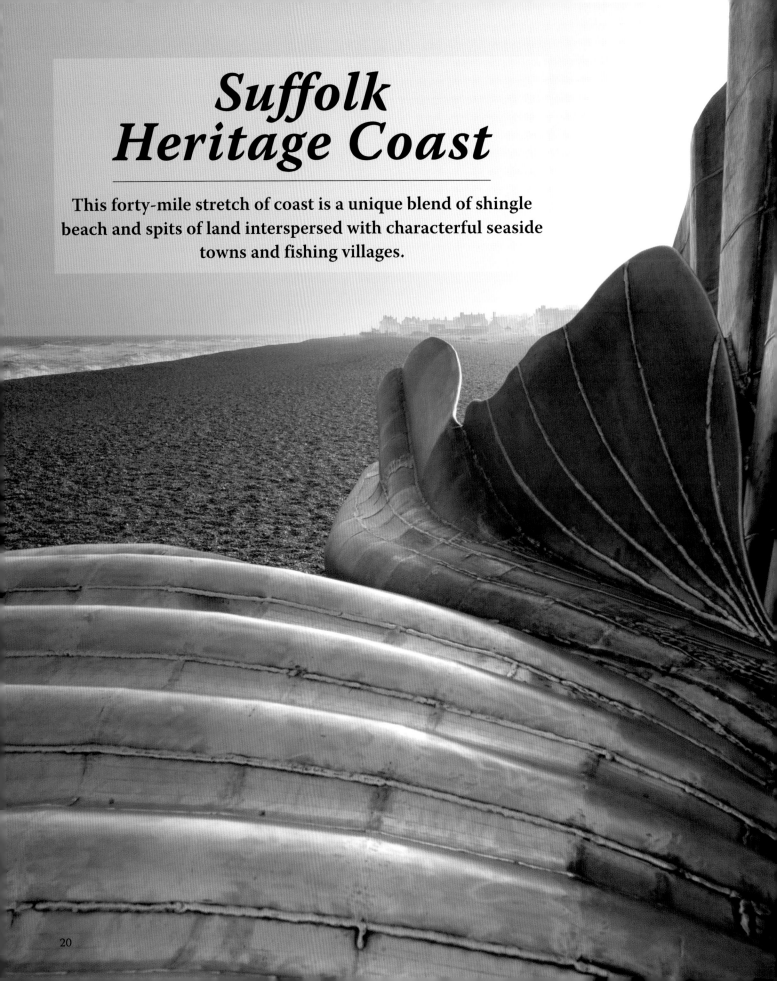

Suffolk Heritage Coast

This forty-mile stretch of coast is a unique blend of shingle beach and spits of land interspersed with characterful seaside towns and fishing villages.

The long and steeply shelved shingle beach at Aldeburgh is dotted with working boats and fishing huts. More recently a modern sculpture entitled *Scallop* by the artist Maggi Hambling has been sited on the beach. It is dedicated to Benjamin Britten who made his home in Aldeburgh and whose opera *Peter Grimes* draws inspiration from a poem by local poet George Crabbe. The seafront has changed little since Victorian times although it has often suffered from the encroaching North Sea. The distinctive 16th-century Moot Hall, on the seafront, now houses a small museum. The majestic 15th-century parish church of St Peter and St Paul's contains the grave of Benjamin Britten and the bust of George Crabbe, born in the town in 1794. Sadly Crabbe's house at nearby Slaughden has long been lost to the sea.

ORFORD A few hundred years ago the estuary of the river Alde was just south of Aldeburgh. Over time, silting up of the river mouth diverted its path and created a spit between the river and sea stretching for over 10 miles down the coast towards Orford, enclosing the estuaries of both the river Alde and the river Ore. This has created a long stretch of sheltered water which is perfect for sailing and boating. The majestic church of St Bartholomew the Apostle (above and below) stands at the top of the village street. It was largely rebuilt in the 14th century.

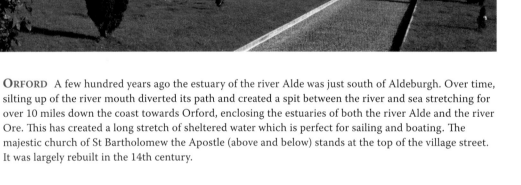

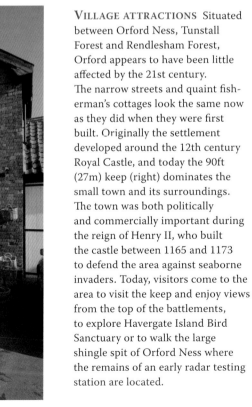

VILLAGE ATTRACTIONS Situated between Orford Ness, Tunstall Forest and Rendlesham Forest, Orford appears to have been little affected by the 21st century. The narrow streets and quaint fisherman's cottages look the same now as they did when they were first built. Originally the settlement developed around the 12th century Royal Castle, and today the 90ft (27m) keep (right) dominates the small town and its surroundings. The town was both politically and commercially important during the reign of Henry II, who built the castle between 1165 and 1173 to defend the area against seaborne invaders. Today, visitors come to the area to visit the keep and enjoy views from the top of the battlements, to explore Havergate Island Bird Sanctuary or to walk the large shingle spit of Orford Ness where the remains of an early radar testing station are located.

SNAPE MALTINGS is a unique cluster of 19th-century malthouses and granaries nestling beside the river Alde five miles inland from Aldeburgh. The site houses the 800-seat world-class concert hall which hosts the famous annual Aldeburgh Music Festival. Other historic buildings on the site are now galleries, shops and restaurants. A tragic fire destroyed the first concert hall in 1969 but it was rebuilt in time for the following year's festival. In 1979, the adjacent barley store was converted into the Britten-Pears School, commemorating composer Benjamin Bitten and his partner the singer Peter Pears. The nearby quay, built to accommodate barges bringing coal to the maltings and carrying malt to breweries, is now lined with pleasurecraft and boats offering pleasure trips down the river Alde.

SNAPE CHURCH The church of St John the Baptist stands on high ground approximately one mile north of the village and a short walk from the Maltings. Originally the building was thatched. The nave was built in the 13th century and the tower and porch added in the 15th century. Inside the church is one of the most beautiful fonts in the county. The village sign reflects the history of Snape – from the Benedictine monks at the ancient Priory of St Mary to the curlew which symbolises the inspirations of the composer Benjamin Britten who loved the sea, the marshes and the countryside around the river Alde.

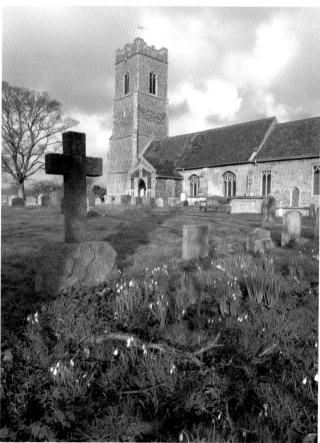

SIZEWELL BEACH

Sizewell Nuclear Power Station (left) owned by British Energy, dominates the Suffolk coast in this region. There are two power plants on the site – Sizewell A which was built in the 1960s and Sizewell B constructed between 1988 and 1995. For 10 years the two plants have supplied almost 3% of the UK's entire electricity needs, and Sizewell B is one of the largest employers in the county and the UK's only large pressurised water reactor. Sizewell A is in the process of being decommissioned. The colours of the station were carefully chosen to blend in with the environment by the Commission of Fine Arts.

THORPENESS Situated two miles north of Aldeburgh on the Suffolk coast, the village of Thorpeness (above) was created as a model seaside resort in the 1900s by Scottish landowner and playwright G Stuart Ogilvie who bought the fishing hamlet of Thorpe and developed it. The weatherboarded turret postmill (left), which sits on top of its matching roundhouse, was originally built in 1803 at nearby Aldringham as a corn mill, but later moved to Thorpeness in 1923. Today the roundhouse is home to a local history collection. The metal-framed building seen in the distance (below) is part water tower, part house; the house was incorporated into the design since locals thought that a plain water tower might be unsightly. It is now known as "The House in the Clouds", one of Suffolk's most famous follies.

North Suffolk Coast

Traditional holiday resorts and pretty inland towns characterise the beautiful coastline of North Suffolk.

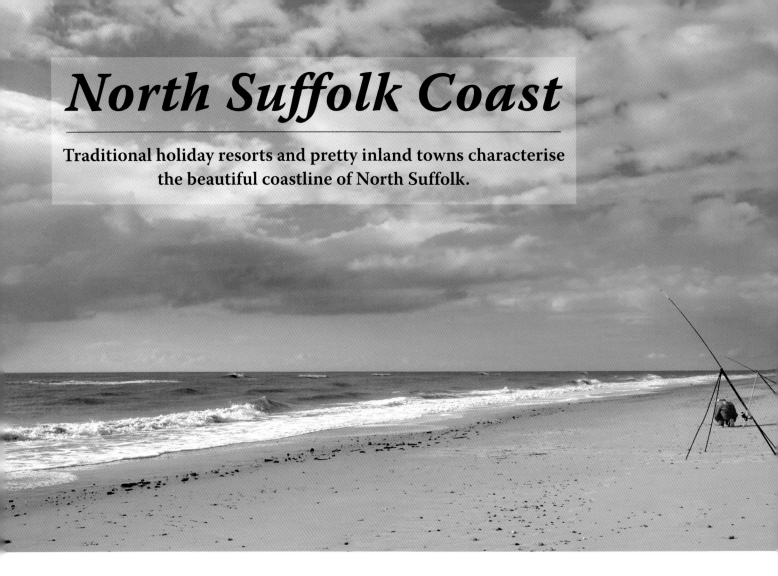

Southwold, a unique and elegant seaside town, has an atmosphere and charm that is quintessentially English. A favourite holiday destination for thousands of visitors each year, the town and surrounding district have many attractions. Bounded by the North Sea to the east, the river Blyth and Southwold harbour to the south-west, and Buss Creek to the north, Southwold is virtually an island. The surrounding countryside is picturesque with many pretty villages. The river Blyth estuary is popular for boating, with its reed beds and saltings, woodlands, open heaths and gently rolling farmland. Fishing was the town's main industry for over 900 years, with herring being particularly important. In the past catches were so good that there was a tithe levied on fish to be paid to the local parish. Southwold's maritime history is preserved at the Sailor's Reading Room, one of the town's four splendid museums. To the north of the High Street lies the church of St Edmund, one of Suffolk's grandest churches.

SOUTHWOLD ATTRACTIONS The resort has over 300 beautifully painted beach huts which evolved from fishermen's and bathers' huts. Today they change hands for high sums. The huts are lifted from the beach each autumn by a giant crane in order to be safe from high tides. The tall white tower of the lighthouse (top) is a notable landmark in the centre of the town; constructed in 1887 it replaced three local lighthouses threatened by coastal erosion.

WALBERSWICK Just across the river Blyth from Southwold, Walberswick was once a thriving trading port dealing in fish, bacon, cheese, corn and timber. The town's prosperity is reflected in the magnificent St Andrews church (right) which stands at the top of the village. Today Walberswick is a popular destination with a pretty harbour and a village green surrounded by quaint houses. A ferryboat across the river links the town with Southwold to the north. To the south lie the wooded heaths of Dunwich and the Minsmere Bird Sanctuary. The resort is famous for hosting the British Open Crabbing Championships each year when hundreds of competitors try to haul as many crabs as they can from the waters of the estuary. Over the years Walberswick has attracted many artists, including Wilson Steer and Charles Rennie Mackintosh.

BLYTHBURGH Surrounded by beautiful countryside, Blythburgh is a small village four miles from the North Sea at Southwold. With a tidal river, heathland, marshes and woods, the area is a magnet for wildlife enthusiasts and birdwatchers. The village is famous for its magnificent parish church, the Holy Trinity (above) which towers over the estuary and is known as "The Cathedral of The Marshes". Over the years the church has suffered from a series of disasters, both man-made and natural. The steeple has been struck by lightning, the interior was damaged by Puritans during the Civil War, and for long periods the church was neglected. Now beautifully restored, it is often used as a venue for concerts during the Aldeburgh Summer Festival.

The photograph of Blythburgh Marshes (above right) captures the distinct character of the Suffolk coastal estuaries. They are at the heart of a Site of Special Scientific Interest and are internationally important for wildlife, in particular for wintering waders and wildfowl. They are often fringed by saltmarsh plants which have adapted to the tough conditions.

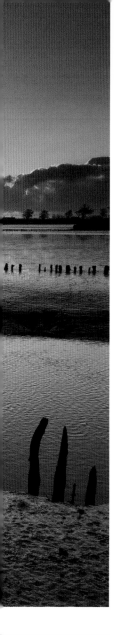

DUNWICH Once the capital of East Anglia, Dunwich was a major trading, fishing and shipbuilding centre with a population of over 3,000. But like so many other settlements along the East Anglian coast, coastal erosion gradually took its toll and much of the town was lost to the sea. Dunwich once had eight churches and almost all had to be abandoned as the sea advanced inland. It is said that it is sometimes possible to hear the sound of church bells coming up from the depths of the sea on quiet nights. Today the village lies between the heath to the north and Minsmere to the south. It consists of a row of Victorian cottages, a church, a small museum and a ruined priory. The steep shingle banks fronting the settlement provide natural flood defences and help reduce the erosive power of the waves. Fishermen still launch their boats from the beach, as they have done traditionally for centuries. Two or three gravestones are all that mark the site of All Saints church, which was abandoned in the late 1700s but which only fell into the sea in the Edwardian period. Dunwich Heath is part of a plateau (known locally as the Sandlings) which once stretched from north Suffolk all the way to Ipswich. Managed by the National Trust it is an ideal place for walkers and birdwatchers to gain an insight into local history, geology and the unique marshland of the area.

Rural Suffolk

Away from the coast, Suffolk has a host of historic market towns and beautiful villages.

The beautiful medieval village of Lavenham lies a few miles north-east of Sudbury and is famous for its collection of half-timbered buildings. During the late middle ages it was one of the wealthiest towns in Britain thanks to the prosperity of the local wool trade. The Guildhall of Corpus Christi (above right) overlooks the market square and was established in 1592 by one of the three wool guilds set up in the town to regulate the industry. The lavish church of St Peter and St Paul (far right), which stands like a sentinel on a hilltop at one end of the high street, was rebuilt in the 15th century to celebrate the Tudor triumph at Bosworth Field. It has a 141ft (43m) tower – the tallest village church tower in Britain.

WOODBRIDGE Situated on the river Deben, not far from the coast, Woodbridge is famous for its superb Tide Mill – one of only four in the country. Sutton Hoo, just across the river, is the burial place of Saxon kings. The story of this remarkable discovery is chronicled in the Woodbridge Museum. During the early 7th century East Anglia flourished under its ruler, Redwald of Rendlesham. When he died he was interred at Sutton Hoo, one of Britain's most important and atmospheric archaeological sites, the burial ground of the Anglo-Saxon kings of East Anglia. The site is now owned by the National Trust and there is a superb visitor centre and exhibition hall. The beautiful Tide Mill (below) was a working mill until 1957 when its oak shaft broke. In 1982 it was fully restored and opened to the public. The splendid Shire Hall (right) stands in the town centre, in the middle of Market Hill. It was built in 1575 by Thomas Seckford, Master of the Court of Requests to Queen Elizabeth 1. The grand church of St Mary's (left), with its magnificent north porch, is one of England's greatest churches. Rebuilt in the 15th century, the best view of its fine tower can be had from the quay. Woodbridge is famous for the variety of elegant Georgian doors which grace many of its splendid buildings. Marston, Gordon and Cumberland Streets, in the centre of the town, have some particularly fine examples.

CLARE A beautiful small Suffolk market town situated between Melford and Haverhill on the north bank of the river Stour, Clare developed as a centre for the wool trade in the Middle Ages. The panoramic rooftop view of the town (above) can be seen from the castle mound situated in Clare country park just two minutes walk from the town centre. The mound has remnants of the old stone castle keep and close by are the old railway track and station – the only railway line in the country ever to have been built inside castle grounds. The impressive roof and spire of the church of St Peter and St Paul is visible throughout the town, towering over the red-topped roofs of the houses clustered around. Many of the old houses in Clare are famous for their pargetting – a rough-cast decorative plasterwork applied to the outside walls, typical of many old buildings in this part of East Anglia. A prime example of this is the Ancient House Museum on the High Street with its collection illustrating the history of the town. This is the start of the local town trail, which takes in Clare Priory. Now the local Catholic church and retreat centre, Clare Priory housed the first order of Augustinian monks in England.

FRAMLINGHAM Situated 18 miles north-east of Ipswich, Framlingham has an attractive market square, Market Hill (left) which features the old water pump used to fill water carts when houses in the town lacked their own supply. The castle (above) is a magnificent landmark with dramatic views across the mere. The sturdy battlements have 13 towers linked by a curtain wall. The castle has an intriguing and chequered history and over the years has been used as a fortress, an Elizabethan prison, a school and poorhouse. It was at Framlingham that Mary Tudor was proclaimed Queen of England following the death of her father, Henry VIII.

SAXTEAD GREEN

WINDMILL Dating from 1776 this elegant and beautifully restored white windmill is a fine example of a traditional Suffolk post mill in full working order. Located approximately two miles north-west of Framlingham, the mill stands prominently in the surrounding flat country-side. Owned by English Heritage it is open to the public between April to October. There has been a post mill at Saxtead Green since 1287 but the current mill is the third to have been built on the site. The mill ceased working commercially in 1947 when the last miller died.

Cambridge & Surrounds

At the heart of the Fens, this ancient university town boasts beautiful architecture in a pastoral setting on the river Cam.

The county town and home of the famous university, Cambridge is one of the busiest tourist spots in Britain. But the city still manages to retain the air of a bustling market town thanks to its narrow streets and the green meadows which extend into the heart of the college area. The sight of punts on the river Cam, glorious college architecture, May balls and the throng of cyclists all help to give Cambridge a romantic air that is almost unique amongst British cities.

THE UNIVERSITY The city centre is dominated by many of the university's historic buildings. Cambridge is the second oldest university in the English-speaking world. The School of Pythagoras, one of the first educational establishments in Cambridge, was founded in 1200, and the building still stands in the grounds of St John's College. King's College was founded in 1441 by Henry VI. It is a superb example of Gothic architecture and its famous chapel is home to the renowned King's College choir, whose Christmas Eve service is broadcast around the world. No visit to Cambridge is complete without a trip in a punt along the river Cam (left). These traditional flat-bottomed boats were used widely in the Fens, the marshy flat lands north of the city and were introduced as pleasure-craft to the town in Edwardian times. Clare College (below) is the second oldest of the Cambridge colleges, and was founded in 1326. It has an enviable, idyllic and peaceful location with extensive riverside gardens. The gardens form part of the famous Backs – the rear part of those colleges which border the beautiful river Cam.

CAMBRIDGE CITY LIFE The centre of Cambridge is packed with historic buildings, many of which are part of the university. The Baron of Beef pub (left), in Bridge Street, a short walk from Magdalene Bridge, is one of the most historic pubs in the city. It first opened in 1752 and its distinctive name refers to a "large, double slice of beef". The market (above) takes place in front of the University Church. The church clock was installed in 1793 and shortly afterwards two Cambridge students composed its chime, subsequently used by Big Ben in London and famous the world over as the "Westminster chime". The photograph (right) is of King's College.

GRANTCHESTER A favourite walk from Newnham on the south-west side of Cambridge is to follow the path along the river Cam upstream for approximately two miles until you reach the open countryside of the famous Grantchester Meadows which extend on both sides of the river. A little further on you reach the village of Grantchester itself, with its famous Orchard Tea Gardens (below) and the old village mill pond (left). Visitors can travel from Cambridge to Grantchester (a distance of 2.5 miles) by punt.

ORCHARD TEA GARDEN The famous Orchard Tea Garden and the adjoining Old Vicarage will forever be associated with the Cambridge poet Rupert Brooke (1887-1915). As an undergraduate, Brooke would often walk with friends to Grantchester and visit Mrs Stevenson of Orchard House who had a small business serving refreshments to visitors beneath the fruit trees at the rear of her home. These trips made such an impression on the young Brooke that after leaving Cambridge, he moved to the Old Vicarage next door to the Orchard. Over the next few years, Brooke's reputation as a poet grew and he found himself at the centre of a literary circle known as the Grantchester Group. Brooke died at the early age of 27 of blood poisoning on the way to fight at the Battle of Gallipoli. His statue (right) now stands in front of the Old Vicarage. Brooke's poem, *The Old Vicarage, Grantchester* referring to the tea room and the church of St Andrew and St Mary in the village ends with these words:

> *Stands the church clock at ten to three?*
> *And is there honey still for tea?*

St Neots The largest town in Cambridgeshire, St Neots is situated on the Great Ouse, which meanders peacefully through the town and forms the border with the historic county of Huntingdonshire. The town owes its development to both God and Mammon. It was the site of a medieval priory built to house the remains of the Cornish monk, Neot, who had been canonised for his work in helping the poor; his bones were brought to the settlement in order to attract pilgrims and a market developed. The growing town received its market charter in 1130 and continued to flourish but the priory did not survive Dissolution. Today the tower of the parish church of St Mary (left) known as the "cathedral of Huntingdonshire" dominates St Neots which regularly plays host to an enticing French market. A mosaic to St Neot is at the heart of the bustling market square.

Cathedral City

The tower of the Cathedral Church of Ely, known as the 'ship of the Fens', soars high above this elegant market town.

ELY CATHEDRAL Completed in 1189, the cathedral is a remarkable example of Romanesque architecture and "the Octagon", an eight-sided tower in the centre of the church (right), is the only Gothic dome in existence. The cathedral is set within the walls of a Benedictine monastery. Today it is particularly famous for its choir and organ music. Housed in the south transept of the cathedral is the famous Stained Glass Museum. This magnificent collection has works of art from 1,300 years of British glass manufacture and includes works by Raphael, William Morris and John Piper. In the shadow of the cathedral is Oliver Cromwell's house, which also houses the Ely Tourist Information Centre. It is the only remaining home other than Hampton Court where Oliver Cromwell and his family are known to have lived. Cromwell was born close by in Huntingdon and in 1666 he moved with his family to the house where they lived for 10 years - the period during which Cromwell served as Lord Protector. The Maltings Quayside area, sited on the banks of the Great River Ouse (below) has been redeveloped from a brewery which dates from 1868. This stretch of river is used by the Cambridge University crew to practise every year for the famous Oxford and Cambridge Boat Race.

Historic Norfolk

Norfolk boasts fine country houses, ancient castles and monuments and an important site of religious pilgrimage.

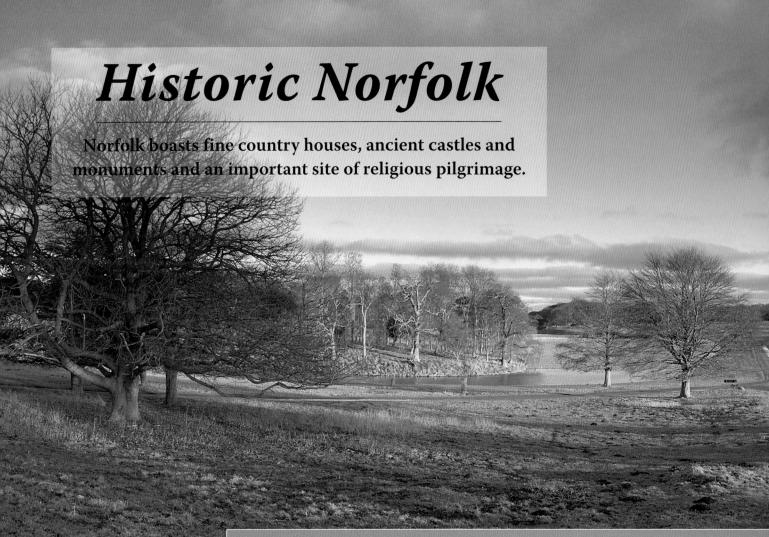

Houghton Hall (right) is a fine Palladian mansion built by Sir Robert Walpole between 1722-1735. He was Britain's first prime minister and served in the reign of George I and George II. The architects were Colen Campbell and James Gibbs. The house was built by Thomas Ripley, and the huge and imposing stable block by William Kent, who also supervised the elaborate and ornate interior decorations. The Walpoles – a landowning family from the villages of Walpole St Peter and Walpole Cross Keys, just west of King's Lynn – came to the area as lords of the manor in 1307.

HOUGHTON HALL The hall is set in 350 acres of fine parkland and gardens in which a large herd of rare, white fallow deer roam freely. The unusual tower cupola (right) complete with weather vane and sundials is mounted above one of the twin side buildings on either side of the main house. An unusual feature of the house is its Toy Soldier Museum. This was established by the 6th Marquess, Lord Cholmondley, who was awarded the Military Cross for valour during the Second World War. It consists of over 20,000 model soldiers and large scenes of the Battle of Waterloo and other famous conflicts. There is also a newly restored five-acre walled garden.

HOLKHAM HALL This beautiful 18th-century Palladian-style country house was built between 1734 and 1762 for Thomas Coke, First Earl of Leicester, on his return from his Grand Tour of Europe. The house (above) is set in 300 acres of magnificent landscaped parkland just west of Wells-next-the-Sea and has remained substantially unchanged since its completion. Among the highlights of the building are the ceiling of the spectacular 50ft high Marble Hall (mostly constructed from alabaster) which is from a design by Inigo Jones, and the opulent salon where paintings by Rubens, Van Dyke and many others are on display. The park has its own five-mile seafront and a herd of 600 fallow deer. In 1776 the newly completed house was passed on to Thomas William Coke (1754-1842), after the death of his father. Thomas was the MP for Norfolk for over 50 years and became famous as one of Britain's greatest ever agricultural reformers.

CASTLE ACRE The picturesque and peaceful village of Castle Acre a few miles north of Swaffham is famous for the twin ruins of Castle Acre castle and Castle Acre priory. This is one of the best examples of a planned Norman settlement anywhere in the country. After visiting the French monastery of Cluny William the Conqueror and his wife Gundrada were so impressed that they vowed to introduce the Cluniac order of monks to England. The priory they founded around 1090 at Castle Acre rapidly developed into one of the largest in the country. Today some of the priory lies in ruins (below right) but much of the original building, including the prior's house and private chapel, still stand making it one of the best preserved monastic sites in England. The impressive castle was built by William De Warenne, first Earl of Surrey and a close supporter of William. Its remains (right) consist of huge earth banks surrounding

a bailey; at one end stands a motte and the remains of a keep. The castle was used until the death of the last Warenne earl in 1347. The original and impressive stone bailey gatehouse which was used as an entrance to the castle stands in the centre of the village. The village of Castle Acre (above) contains a large number of flint and cobble cottages centred on Stocks Green, the attractive green planted with large lime trees and once the site of the village stocks.

GREAT MASSINGHAM

GREAT MASSINGHAM

A picture postcard village east of King's Lynn, Great Massingham has an enormous village green and several attractive large ponds, some of which were used as fishponds for the 11th century Augustinian abbey which once stood here. The twin village of Little Massingham lies a few miles to the north. The great square tower of St Mary's church (above) dominates the village skyline and houses four bells. The church has a magnificent 13th century porch. Once a year the church is used to display artefacts associated with the now disused Massingham airfield to the east of the village, a centre of bomber command during the Second World War. The village sign represents Great Massingham's agricultural heritage and its former 11th century Augustinian abbey. The Peddars Way trail links this area with the coastal villages of north Norfolk and passes to the west of the village.

WALPOLE ST PETER

The magnificent church (left) at Walpole St Peter is one of the finest in England. Known as "the Cathedral of the Fenlands", it is hidden away in the countryside between Holbeach and King's Lynn, just south of the A17 into north Norfolk. Once Walpole St Peter and Walpole St Andrew were two separate villages but they are now linked into one settlement. The famous 13th century church hosts a spectacular annual flower festival and welcomes visitors from all over the country. The great landowning family the Walpoles hailed from the villages of Walpole St Peter and Walpole Cross Keys (a few miles to the north) and Sir Robert Walpole (1676-1745), whose life's work was the creation of the great mansion at Houghton Hall, became Britain's first Prime Minister. Walpole Water Gardens are a superb attraction. The garden has been designed and landscaped by the Norfolk-born artist Peter Cousins.

BIRCHAM The restored windmill (right) in Great Bircham, a village a few miles north-east of King's Lynn, is a great attraction for visitors. The village is set amidst gently rolling fertile farmland typical of this area of north Norfolk. At one time this part of East Anglia had over 300 mills grinding corn for animal feed and bread-making. Today very few mill buildings remain and most of those are in ruins. Dating from 1846, Bircham has been restored and is the only mill in the area in working order and open to the public. Visitors can climb all five floors to the fan stage where there are panoramic views of the surrounding countryside. The church of St Mary the Virgin, in the centre of the village, is well known for its peal of bells and one of its ancient bells is on display in the nave of the church.

LITTLE WALSINGHAM This village has been a place of religious pilgrimage since the 11th century when a vision of the Virgin Mary appeared to a local noblewoman. It is often described as "England's Nazareth". Over the years, millions of pilgrims have followed the procession from the parish church of St Mary (above) to the Abbey grounds where the shrine of Our Lady of Walsingham is housed. They traditionally walk the mile and a half to the Slipper Chapel where pilgrims leave their shoes before walking on to the Holy House. St Mary's is a magnificent building. The interior of the church is spacious and lavishly decorated. The superb Seven Sacrament octagonal font, common in East Anglian churches, has been exquisitely crafted. It is held in such high regard that a plaster replica was taken to the Great Exhibition of 1851. The quaint streets in the village of Little Walsingham are full of medieval and Georgian houses. The old weathered door (right) is to be found on the medieval water pump in the centre of the village.

Royal Country

The Sandringham Estate lies close to Castle Rising, a few miles inland from Norfolk's beautiful west coast.

SANDRINGHAM The beautiful country retreat of the Queen and the Duke of Edinburgh has been passed down through four generations of British monarchs. By 1870, the original Georgian house had been completely remodelled. Sandringham House, its museum, church and gardens are open to the public and each year thousands of visitors

flock to the Sandringham Flower Show. The gardens cover 60 acres and are home to rare and historic trees, together with King George VI's garden, designed by Sir Geoffrey Jellicoe, two large lakes and a stream walk as well as Queen Alexandra's Nest, the charming summerhouse perched above Sandringham's upper lake. The royal family usually spend Christmas at Sandringham and remain there officially until February. The house and the surrounding area is much loved by the royal family: George V (1865-1936) wrote, "Dear old Sandringham, the place I love better than anywhere else in the world". The church of St Mary Magdalene (left) dates from the 16th century. George VI died, aged 56, at Sandringham in February 1952. The king's coffin lay in the church before being removed to Windsor for interment. Shown here are the primary school (above) and church clock (right) in the nearby estate village of West Newton.

ANMER The tiny village of Anmer has an enviable location, situated midway between Sandringham and Houghton Hall in north Norfolk. It is a place where time seems to stand still – except, of course, when a keenly contested bowls match is taking place on the green beside the sports and social club. The main street is lined with attractive flint and redbrick cottages. In the past, most of the inhabitants of the village worked on the Royal estate or at nearby Anmer Hall. The church of St Mary was built around the time when the great family of Calthorp were Lords of the Manor. Anmer passed from the Calthorps to the Coldham family in 1678 and memorials to the Coldhams can be seen inside the church, which is just visible through a huge canopy of mature trees. The parish now covers about 1,400 acres and is part of the Royal Estate at Sandringham; virtually all the houses in the village belong to the Sandringham Estate which also includes the local villages of Wolferton, West Newton, Appleton, Flitcham and Sherbourne.

The small church of St Mary lies close to Anmer Hall and contains beautiful stained-glass windows (right).
The church was a particular favourite of Queen Mary, the wife of George V.

BLICKLING HALL One of England's finest Jacobean houses, famous for its long gallery, fine furniture, superb library, pictures and tapestries, Blickling Hall is a short distance north-west of Aylsham. The house was built on the site of a former manor house and was once home to Anne Boleyn, the wife of Henry VIII and the mother of Elizabeth I. Legend has it that her ghost haunts the house. Today, Blickling, which is surrounded by stunning scenery and parkland, is owned by the National Trust; it was first opened to

the public in 1962. The gardens consist of three separate areas – the Jacobean Garden, the Georgian Garden and the Lothian Garden, named after the eighth Marquess of Lothian and his wife Constance. The house was requisitioned during the second world war and used as the officers mess for nearby RAF Oulton.

Norfolk's West Coast

Facing the wide expanse of the Wash, the west coast is famous
for its panoramic sunsets over the sea.

SNETTISHAM South of Hunstanton on the north Norfolk coast, Snettisham is a pretty village with an RSPB nature reserve two miles to the west. The village looks across the Wash towards Lincolnshire and is one of the best places in Britain to see spectacular flocks of migrating birds on the move. In the depths of winter, at dawn and dusk, thousands of pink-footed geese commute between their safe roosts in the Wash and nearby farmland where they feed on the remnants of the sugar beet harvest. The birds make an eerie sound – rather like the sound of an approaching steam train. At high tide, when the sea water covers large areas of the mudflats of the Wash, thousands of wading birds take flight and move away from their feeding grounds onto the surrounding islands and mud banks. The RSPB have provided hides from which this spectacle can be viewed. The Country Park is a popular venue for visitors with a host of attractions including a unique deer park.

HEACHAM Situated on the coast between King's Lynn and the seaside resort of Hunstanton, Heacham has two beaches, one to the north and one to the south. Both face west and are ideal locations from which to enjoy panoramic views across the Wash. The view (above) was taken out of season in a strong, almost gale force wind. On the eastern side of the village is England's oldest lavender farm (right) based at Caley Mill. With more than 100 acres under cultivation, the intoxicating scent of lavender drifts in the air for miles around. The farm hosts an annual Lavender Festival every July when the crop is harvested and distilled.

HUNSTANTON "Sunny Hunny", as Hunstanton is often called, is 15 miles east of King's Lynn and has some of the best surf on the east coast of Norfolk. It is a traditional English seaside resort with many attractions, including a sea life centre, a funfair, amusement arcades, leisure centre and an aquarium.

The picturesque village of Old Hunstanton, just east of Hunstanton, has a medieval church, two pitch and putt golf courses, a championship golf course, coastal footpaths and a nature reserve. The town's most prominent landmark is the Old Lighthouse (left). Beacons or lantern lights have been used to warn shipping of dangers along this coast for centuries and the first lighthouse was built in 1666. The present building was constructed in 1844.

HUNSTANTON CLIFFS Close to the promenade and Beach Terrace Road in Hunstanton lie these distinctive and eye-catching striped cliffs (right). This spectacular formation is a graphic display of Britain's geology over many millions of years. Fossils can be found in both the white and red chalk and it is not unusual, particularly at weekends, to find groups of fossil-hunters armed with hammers and chisels trying to prise specimens from the cliff face.

HOLME NEXT THE SEA Holme is an unspoilt coastal village, sited at the point where the 46 mile (74km) long-distance footpath known as the Peddars Way reaches its northern seaward end. The Norfolk Coastal Path that follows the coast from Hunstanton to Cromer can also be accessed here. The photographs (left and below) taken in winter, illustrate the beauty and remote location of this coastal area which has been designated an area of outstanding natural beauty. The shifting sand dunes are covered in marram grass which helps reduce drifting in the strong winds. An ancient timber circle, consisting of 55 oak trunks, was discovered in 1999 on Holme beach. Dubbed "seahenge", it dates from 2049 BC and is now on display at the refurbished Lynn Museum at nearby King's Lynn. The church of St Mary (right), with its square 15th-century tower, is a distinctive landmark in the area.

It has a simple but austere interior with three baptismal fonts, a beautiful organ and many striking memorials. The churchyard contains a number of graves of the Nelson family who lived nearby in Holme House. Admiral Horatio Nelson, a descendant of one of the sons of the family, spent his boyhood years in nearby Burnham Thorpe.

Nelson Country

Britain's greatest naval commander was born in Burnham Thorpe and his boyhood years were spent on the creeks of Norfolk's north coast.

The three villages of Brancaster, Brancaster Staithe and Burnham Deepdale form a more or less continuous line along the marshland fringing Brancaster Bay. At low tide a petrified forest can be seen on the shoreline. The sheltered inlet at Brancaster Staithe was the ideal location for a harbour, and the Romans built a fort here and gave the name *Branodunum* to the area. The fort defended the coast from marauding Saxon and Frankish pirates; the garrison was manned by troops from present-day Croatia and Montenegro. Legend has it that England's greatest naval commander, Nelson, sailed his first boat at Brancaster Staithe.

BRANCASTER The Royal West Norfolk Golf Course at Brancaster is described in its brochure as being "close to the beach". This is certainly an apt description of this view near the clubhouse (below) looking north at first light in January. The open skies, attractive unspoilt countryside and sea air make this stretch of coast popular with golfers and there are courses at Hunstanton, Sheringham, Fakenham, King's Lynn and Castle Rising. The vast area of saltmarsh, intertidal mud and sandflats at Brancaster is an area of outstanding natural beauty; over 4.5 miles of this coastline is owned by the National Trust. The sandy beach, fringed in part by beautiful sand dunes, is ideal for family holidays, beachcombing and birdwatching. The area is an important breeding ground for birds: nearby, a private ferry runs from Burnham Overy Staithe to the National Nature Reserve on Scolt Island. The view of the Tower Mill (right) at Burnham Overy Staithe is attractively framed by chicory plants growing along the edge of the surrounding cornfields.

THE BURNHAMS This cluster of villages centres around the pretty town of Burnham Market (right), near the Norfolk coast. The town has attracted many new residents in recent years but still remains relatively unspoiled, and it is pleasant to travel along the quiet lanes a stone's throw from the coast. Here the verges and hedgerows explode with summer flowers, providing an excellent habitat for wildlife. Just over a mile to the north-west is Burnham Thorpe, the birthplace of Lord Nelson. The old rectory in which the young Horatio was born was demolished after his father's death but it is marked by a plaque. The bust of Nelson (above) is located in the chancel of All Saints church where his father was rector.

BURNHAM OVERY STAITHE

Sailing is immensely popular at Burnham Overy Staithe (above and right) and enthusiasts can check on the weather and tides by means of a webcam sited on top of the boathouse, which gives a north-easterly view of the Norfolk marshes and the sand dunes of Gun Hill. The boathouse is a traditional chandlery offering boat storage and repairs, waterproof clothing and gifts. Flagstaff House, a local self-catering holiday cottage, was once the home of Captain Woodget, master of the tea clipper *Cutty Sark*, which is now in dry dock at Greenwich in south-east London.

North Norfolk Heritage Coast

Between Holme next the Sea and Weybourne is a landscape of saltmarsh and sand dunes, interspersed with historic villages.

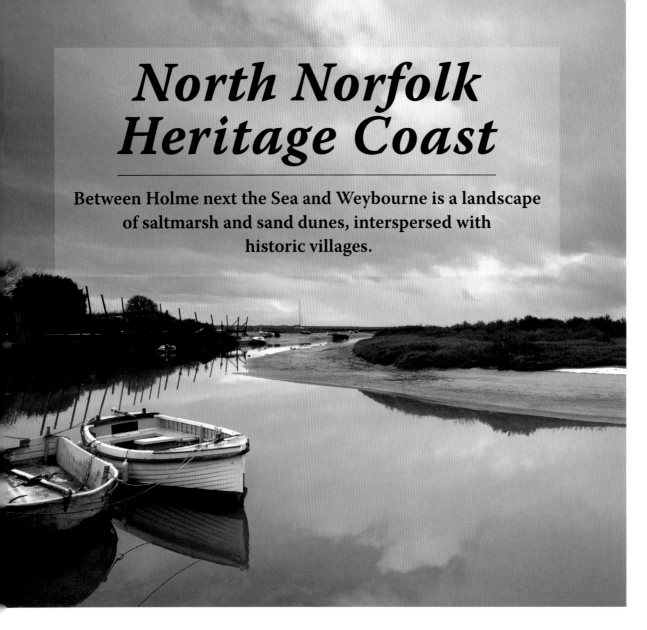

In the Middle Ages, this much-loved coastal village was a busy commercial port. Today, the estuary has silted up and only smaller boats can weave their way through the marshes. Owned by the National Trust since 1912, Blakeney Point is a 3.5 mile sand and shingle spit which can only be reached by boat or by walking along the beach from Cley. It is one of Britain's foremost bird sanctuaries and is also famous for its seal colonies (right). There are approximately 500 seals in this mixed colony and boats are able to get remarkably close to the seals without seeming to disturb their normal sleepy demeanour.

WELLS-NEXT-THE-SEA

One of the most attractive towns of the north Norfolk coast, relatively unaffected by over-commercialisation, Wells-next-the-Sea is a charming, historic seaside resort brimming with character and atmosphere. Despite its name, the town now stands about a mile from open water. It is packed with historic houses and narrow lanes, or "yards", lead down to the bustling quayside. At low tide the beach seems to stretch to the far horizon and there are striking views to the west towards Holkham and Burnham Overy Staithe. The inland saltmarshes are a haven for wildlife and very popular with birdwatchers. A great attraction for children is the tradition of "gillying" (fishing) for crabs around the quay. The beach (below) is within easy reach of the Holkham Nature reserve. The brightly-painted beach huts are sited close to a stretch of pine woodland beside a long sweeping beach, half a mile from the harbour. The historic Dutch sailing clipper *The Albatros*, one of the oldest sailing ships still afloat, is often moored at the quay.

CLEY-NEXT-THE-SEA The Norfolk coast is renowned for its attractive villages constructed from flint and Cley is arguably one of the finest. The village is sited midway between Wells-next-the-Sea and Cromer. The parish church of St Margaret (below) stands majestically on a grassy knoll above the village green; it is hard to imagine that it once overlooked the harbour mouth of Blakeney Haven – a massive port that stretched west towards the town of Blakeney. The size and scale of the church bears testament to the fact that Cley was a vital port in late medieval England. Wealthy merchants who had prospered as a result of trade with the Low Countries built and rebuilt the church in its grand style over the centuries. Visitors can discover the history of Cley by taking the village trail which goes past the old village forge, the former smokehouse and the post office, which was used as a troop billet in the first world war. The size and scale of the Cley windmill (right), dates from the early 18th century. It overlooks the saltmarshes, Cley bird sanctuary and the sea.

SALTHOUSE Steeped in history and tradition, the village of Salthouse is a magical place. The settlement is made up of a scattering of flint cottages, a post office, an inn and a seafood restaurant. The church of St Nicholas stands in an imposing position overlooking the village and the marshes beyond. It is reached by a track from the shore, lined with flint walls and was built in this lofty position in the 16th century by Sir Henry Heydon to protect it from flooding and to act as a beacon for ships out at sea. The church has beautiful stained-glass windows and, on the choir stalls, graffiti can be seen which dates from the 18th century and depicts the tall-masted sailing ships of the times. Salthouse Marshes (above) are seen here at dusk. They are one of a string of important birding sites along the north Norfolk coast. The area contains a number of fresh and saltwater lagoons, protected to the north by a long and high shingle bank and fringed by marshland to the south. This habitat is ideal for wildlife and particularly for birds. As its name suggests, the village of Salthouse and the nearby marshes were once a centre for salt production. The village was largely made up of warehouses for the storage of salt. The village was inundated during the spring flood of 1953 and many of the old buildings were lost. Traditions die hard in this region and managing and cutting gorse to feed the bake-house is still remembered by some of the elderly residents.

Norfolk Seaside

Charming holiday resorts and pretty inland towns
characterise the beautiful coastline of north Norfolk.

CROMER PIER Piers and jetties have long been part of the history of the attractive seaside resort of Cromer: in 1390, Richard III decreed that the town should be allowed to levy taxes on incoming cargo to pay for a landing stage and pier. In the 19th century two wooden jetties graced the shoreline – the first, built in 1822, was wrecked by a storm and was replaced by a second which was destroyed in 1897 when a coal boat collided with it. The current elegant Edwardian pier celebrated its centenary in 2001 and was one of the first "pleasure" piers to be built in the 20th century. The Pavilion Theatre is a great attraction and provides entertainment all year round plus a traditional end of the pier "Seaside Special" show during the summer season. In 2000 Cromer pier was winner of the "Pier of the Year" award. In competition with the pier as Cromer's best-loved attraction is the Cromer crab, the town's famous culinary delicacy which has been harvested by local fishermen for centuries. Regarded by afficionados as the "king of British crabs", it is the basic ingredient of many local recipes.

CROMER ATTRACTIONS Cromer parish church dominates this beautiful seaside resort. Its spire is 160ft (50m) high; climbing the 172 steps to the top provides visitors with breathtaking views of the town and out to the North Sea. From this lofty perch they can contemplate the fate of the village of Shipden which was swallowed up by the sea during the middle ages; Shipden's church is now reckoned to be at least 437 yards (400m) from the shoreline – a warning if one were needed that coastal erosion has always been problem on this coast. A magnificent mid-summer sunrise with the whole seafront bathed in gentle warm sunshine, is an invitation to sit on one of the benches for a while and enjoy the view.

CROMER HISTORY Cromer's expansion as a seaside resort was hastened in the late Victorian era when a rail link from Norwich and the Midlands led to the construction of many grand hotels. In 1887 the town was so popular that a second railway station, Cromer Beach (now Cromer station), was built close to the seafront. The town was a favourite with wealthy families from Norwich who built summer homes here. King Edward VII visited the resort and played golf here. The London journalist Clement Scott popularised the resort in his writings on the area. Scott dubbed the wealthy Overstrand and Sidestrand villages to the east and south-east of the town "Poppyland" because of the profusion of these flowers growing along the roadside and meadows in the two villages.

SHERINGHAM Fishing was once the lifeblood of this attractive town and today at sunrise fishermen continue to push their boats out to sea from the gap in the cliffs known as "The Hythe", while holidaymakers are still fast asleep dreaming of sunshine, sandy beaches and crab sandwiches. The fishermen store their boats and equipment as their forebears did between Westcliff and the Fishermen's Slope close to the lifeboat shed. In the late 19th century Sheringham boasted over 150 fishing boats; the way of life of this close-knit fishing community is documented in the local museum. Born and bred Sheringham people are termed "Shannocks" and the nicknames of some of the fishermen – Butter Balls, Bread-Alone, Pongo and Teapot – bear testimony to the rich community life enjoyed by the residents of old. Now tourism, which began with the arrival of the railway in 1887, supports the majority of the local community. But the character of the town is nurtured by the Sheringham and District Local Preservation Society, who are restoring the fishing sheds between Westcliff and the Fishermen's Slope.

The Broads

Peat digging over millions of years has created the unique
landscape of this region which straddles the border
of Norfolk and Suffolk.

The large water-filled Broads are connected by over 200 miles of navigable rivers, dykes and cuts. Although this watery region straddles both Norfolk and Suffolk it is known as the Norfolk Broads. There are over 50 Broads but only 13 of them are usually open to the fleets of pleasurecraft which ply these waterways. The Broads, which extend over nearly 75,000 acres, are managed by the Broads Authority and certain areas have been given conservation status, rather like a national park. Hickling Broad (left and above) fringed by vast drifts of reedbeds, presents a particularly evocative Broadland scene complete with a pretty village – split into two parts, Hickling Heath and Hickling Green – and a mooring (or staithe) with traditional reed-thatched boathouses.

HICKLING BOAT-HOUSES
Hickling Broad is the largest of the navigable lakes in the Broads, covering over 14,000 acres. The moorings at Hickling Broad by the Pleasure Boat Inn are a popular port of call and the pretty and secluded village of Hickling Heath is just a short stroll away. The nature reserve here is maintained by the Norfolk Wildlife Trust. The beautiful thatched boathouses were photographed early in February on a bitterly cold morning following a light frost.

HORSEY Horsey Mill (above), a fully restored drainage windpump, has been owned by the National Trust since 1948. It was entirely rebuilt in 1912, and stands proudly beside the edge of Horsey Mere between Sea Palling and Winterton-on-Sea. The redbrick building has five storeys and from the top visitors can enjoy superb views of the Broads and coast. In 1961 the mill was restored but had its "tail" blown off in the great October hurricane of 1987. The church of All Saints (left) stands on a wooded knoll, the only high spot in the area. The exquisite stained-glass window in the church is a commemorative portrait of Catherine Ursula Rising, who died in 1890. She was the wife of Charles Rising, the owner of the Horsey Estate. Catherine is depicted standing by an easel in a room at Horsey Hall.

MARTHAM BROAD The National Nature Reserve at Martham Broad close to Winterton-on-Sea is managed by the Norfolk Wildlife Trust. It can be approached on foot from the staithe at West Somerton and contains rare species such as the swallowtail butterfly and marsh harrier. The heron (below), nature's most accomplished fisherman, was photographed soon after sunrise basking in the early warm sunshine sitting on top of a small tree. In the early middle ages the village of Martham grew to a sizeable settlement of over 1,000 inhabitants due to the fact that the landowner, the bishop of Thetford, Herbert de Losingo, built the cathedral at Norwich and was a patron of the local monastery. The inhabitants of Martham earned a living supplying the monks with food and fuel. Later, from the 17th century onwards, brickmaking became an important activity; many of the older houses in the village feature the famous "Norfolk red bricks" which all have the same appearance, texture and colour. Today, this picture-postcard village with its duckpond is surrounded by pretty houses, many of them thatched.

EAST SOMERTON Blood Hill wind farm (above) is located to the east of Winterton-on-Sea on either side of a minor road that runs from East Somerton towards Gibbet Hill. The 10 turbines (five sited on each side of the road) were constructed in 1992 as one of the first wind farms in Britain. They generate enough power to supply around 1,400 homes. This photograph was taken just after sunrise. The names Blood Hill and Gibbet Hill are a reminder of the area's violent history – a battle took place at Blood Hill between the Saxons and Vikings reputedly so terrible that the surrounding hills ran red with the blood of the two opposing sides.

WEST SOMERTON Boats can moor in the dyke at West Somerton (left), where there is a post office store and the Lion Inn is just five minutes walk from the village staithe. Robert Hales, known as "the Norfolk giant", is buried on the south side of the village church. He was 7ft 8ins and weighed over 32 stone; he appeared at fairs and shows throughout England. The area around the Somertons is a patchwork of gently rolling hills, old traditional windmills, church spires and wind pumps. Visitors can often enjoy the tranquil sight of ships' sails drifting across wide horizons. From the dyke, boats can access the river Thurne which rises close to Martham Broad and then flows for around six miles to Thurne Mouth where it joins the Bure.

HOW HILL The river Ant runs close to the Broadland village of Ludham. Nearby is How Hill House, a magnificent thatched Arts & Crafts country house, famous for its Edwardian gardens and views over the surrounding marshes. The architect Edward Boardman built it as a summer house for his family in 1904 and it became a study centre in 1967. It is surrounded by a 365 acre estate which contains the delightful Toad Hole Cottage Museum. Located in an original marshman's cottage the museum gives visitors an insight into Victorian life on the Broads. There are three restored windmills at How Hill. The evocative Turf Fen windmill (below and right) was erected in 1875 to drain Horning marshes into the river Ant. Close by is a more recent wind pump (below right).

UPTON STAITHE The small village of Upton is situated west of Great Yarmouth on the northern edge of the Broads. Upton Staithe (right) has good cruiser moorings. At low tide the dyke is shallow and it is tricky for boating enthusiasts to navigate between the lines of moored yachts. The village contains the attractive church of St Margaret and a local pub – the White Horse Inn. Near Upton Broad, Upton Fen is managed by the Norfolk Wildlife Trust.

ST OLAVES A few miles south-west of Great Yarmouth lies St Olaves and its near neighbour Herringfleet. The area is the site of three mills: St Olaves Drainage Mill on the east bank of the river Waveney looking up the river from St Olaves Bridge; Mallets Mill which drained the Scales Marshes and was demolished in 1893; and the Smock Drainage Mill which stands a mile south-west of the Norman church of Herringfleet. St Olaves Mill was built around 1910 by Dan England, the Ludham millwright. It also drives a scoop wheel for lifting marsh water from the ditches.

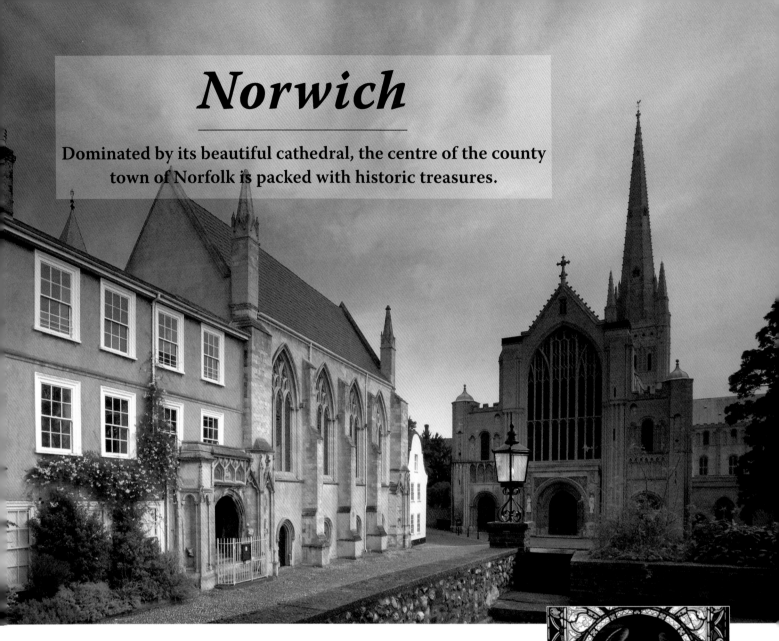

Norwich

Dominated by its beautiful cathedral, the centre of the county town of Norfolk is packed with historic treasures.

Norwich is an ecclesiastical city with over 57 medieval churches built within the city walls, 31 of which are still standing. The magnificent cathedral of the Holy and Undivided Trinity (above) dominates the city centre and is the focus of spiritual life in Norfolk. Founded in 1096 its spire – the second highest in England – soars to 315ft (96m) and makes the cathedral the most distinctive landmark in East Anglia. The roof of the nave is embellished with over one thousand carved bosses that depict biblical characters and scenes from the lives of the saints; this magnificent work of art is considered to be one of the finest treasures of medieval Europe. The cathedral is separated from the busy city streets by sturdy flint walls which protect the cathedral close (above) and create a tranquil oasis for city-dwellers and visitors.

NORWICH CASTLE The castle at Norwich (above) was
originally a wooden motte and bailey construction built by
William the Conqueror in 1067 to serve as his royal palace
in eastern England. Over the years the castle was rebuilt but
now all that exists is the central keep which was clad in Bath
stone by Anthony Salvin between 1835-8. Today the castle
serves as the city museum with exhibits depicting East
Anglian life through the ages, from the time of Boudicca
who fought the Romans, to collections of porcelain and
modern British painting.

CATHEDRAL CLOISTERS The impressive two-storey cloisters (right) built between 1297-1430, are second only in size
to those at Salisbury Cathedral. They replaced the original
cloisters which were destroyed by fire in 1272 during riots
at an annual market fair in the town. They were a key part
of the original Benedictine monastery and even today there
is a sense of the role the cloisters played in the monks' lives
– they were the places in which the monks would read, write
and teach. Doors from the cloisters led to the chapter house,
the dormitory stairs, the infirmary, library, refectory and the
"locutory" where the monks would talk to visitors. This last
room now houses the Cathedral shop.

SWINESHEAD Lincolnshire is one of the most sparsely populated counties in England but the flat arable lands of the Fens are rich in natural resources. The soil in this region is so fertile that three crops can usually be grown in one year. In early spring, fields of daffodils and tulips line the sides of the road near Swineshead, providing travellers in north Norfolk with a colourful tapestry to brighten what could sometimes seem a flat and often bleak and desolate landscape.

First published in 2010 by Myriad Books Limited
35 Bishopsthorpe Road
London SE26 4PA

Photographs and text copyright © 2010 John Potter

John Potter has asserted his right under the Copyright, Designs and Patents Act, 1988, to be identified as the author of this work. All rights reserved. No part of this publication may be reproduced, stored in a retrieval system or transmitted in any form or by any means, electronic, mechanical, photocopying, recording or otherwise without the prior permission of the copyright owners.

ISBN   1 84746 353 3
EAN 978 1 84746 353 1

Designed by Jerry Goldie Graphic Design
Printed in China

www.myriadbooks.com